IF YOU WERE A BAT

written by
Susan McCloskey

illustrated by
Henrik Drescher

HARCOURT BRACE & COMPANY

Orlando Atlanta Austin Boston San Francisco Chicago Dallas New York
Toronto London

If you were a bat, you would
go out every night.
When the sun went down,
off you would fly.

If you were a bat, you might eat bugs.
You would catch them with your feet and your wings.

Open wide!

If you were a bat, you would
go home in the morning.
You would lick your fur coat
to keep it clean.

Then you would sleep all day long. But you would not sleep alone.

Sweet dreams.